Korea

Mongolia

Shanghai

East China Sea

Japan

CHINA

Tropic of Cancer

Pacific

ROUTES

Canton

TAIWAN

Ocean

Hong Kong
Macao

Philippines

BURMA

SIAM

South China

BAY
of
Mandalay

Bengal

Singapore

Sea

Guinea

Ceylon
(Sri Lanka)

SUMATRA

ISLA

Java

OCEAN

SPICE

the ANTIPODES

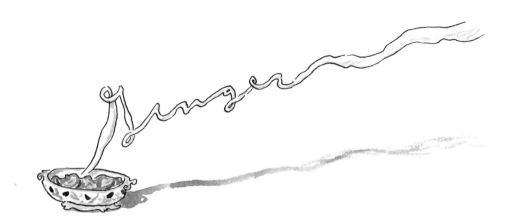

GINGER

by Lou Seibert Pappas

Illustrations by Eric Hanson

CHRONICLE BOOKS
SAN FRANCISCO

Text and recipes copyright © 1996 by Lou Seibert Pappas.
Illustrations copyright © 1996 by Eric Hanson.
All rights reserved.
No part of this book may be reproduced in any form
without written permission from the publisher.

Book and cover design by Sarah Bolles

Library of Congress Cataloging in Publication Data available

Printed in Hong Kong.

ISBN 0-8118-0579-4

Distributed in Canada by
Raincoast Books
8680 Cambie Street
Vancouver, B.C. V6P 6M9

10 9 8 7 6 5 4 3 2 1

Chronicle Books
275 Fifth Street
San Francisco, CA 94103

acknowledgments

❧

With thanks to "Down
Under" cooks Shirley Bradstock,
Alison Hight, and Santini Grilli
for sharing their ginger treats.
Again, thank you Cathie Colson,
for your practical expertise.

contents

preface

Dried, fresh, or crystallized, ginger is a beloved and tantalizing spice. Though hot and spicy, it brings a cooling sensation to the palate. Whatever it touches becomes more vibrant.

My first taste of ginger was as an ingredient in gingerbread cookies, with their plump tummies and bendable arms and legs. Warm gingerbread dolloped with whipped cream skimmed from cream-topped milk bottles was another favorite treat of my childhood.

Fresh ginger was part of my introduction to what was known then as "foreign cooking." Ginger shreds perfumed grilled teriyaki flank steak, whole steamed rockfish, Chinese stir-fries, noodle dishes, and dim sum I savored at Asian restaurants ranging from grand to tiny hole-in-the-wall venues.

When my culinary repertoire expanded into Indian and Moroccan dishes, ginger was there, toning down the heat of curries. Sushi with thin slices of pickled ginger became an addiction that prompted eating these delicious wafers with other foods.

Fresh and crystallized ginger has become more popular over the years in Western and Continental dishes, too, from tropical fruit plates and crème brûlée to ice cream. I soon realized that ginger added zest to such everyday foods as a morning fruit smoothie and bran muffins, and that many salsas, relishes, and chutneys demanded it.

Now a hand of fresh ginger, a jar of ground, and a bag of crystallized slices are essential to my pantry. I hope this book will bring you some new ideas along with some old favorite ways for adding this spice to your life.

introduction

A pungent spice with a warming bite, ginger has been cultivated in tropical Asia for over three thousand years. Though often called *gingerroot*, it is actually a multilobed rhizome, or underground stem. The word *ginger* derives from the Sanskrit *sringavera*, meaning "horn-root," from the resemblance of the misshapen, flattened rhizome to the horns of an animal, according to Waverley Root—and indeed a whole piece of fresh ginger does somewhat resemble an antler. In the food trade, these are spoken of as "hands," or "races," a carryover from *raices*, the Portuguese-Spanish word for "roots."

A ginger plant (*Zingiber officinale*) grows to a height of about three feet and produces beautiful, pale yellow orchidlike blossoms. Though a perennial, usually it is grown as an annual and is propagated by dividing the roots. Plant shoots appear in ten days, and harvest occurs in about seven to ten months.

Although its exact origins are unknown, ginger is native to the hot tropical jungles of Southeast Asia. Phoenician and Arab traders first carried it from Southeast Asia. It was used in the Middle East and southern Europe well before Roman times. Later, the Phoenician sea route was augmented by the overland caravan route, or the Silk Road. The Portuguese then introduced ginger to Africa, and the Spanish took it to the West Indies. By the sixteenth century, the Spaniards had a flourishing Jamaican ginger trade with continental Europe. Today ginger is grown in many tropical countries, including Australia, South America, Indochina, West Africa, Jamaica, Hawaii, and Fiji.

Galangal is a member of the ginger family, yet its flavor is so different from fresh ginger that it cannot be substituted for it. Greater galangal has large spicy knobs and is primarily used in the cuisine of Thailand, where it is known as Thai ginger. Lesser galangal is used more as a vegetable than a spice. The small, fingerlike rhizomes are cooked whole in curries in Southeast Asia.

Once as valuable as a precious gem, in Roman times ginger was expensive—costing fifteen times as much as black pepper—and taxed heavily, although it was plentiful. Lovers of exotic food, the Romans savored it at home and in their colonies in Germany, France, and Britain.

In medieval and Tudor times ginger was particularly popular in England, both as a medicinal and a culinary spice. In *Twelfth Night*, Shakespeare's clown Feste refers to ginger as being "hot i' the mouth." It was thought to be a preventative against the plague and was included in pomanders and potpourris to dispel odors, and was even taken as an aphrodisiac. Ginger became so popular that it had its own canister at the table. Gingerbread was a favorite treat of the time, stamped out with molds and sold at fairs and throughout the country by gingerbread vendors. In the late sixteenth century, Queen Elizabeth I employed a full-time gingerbread baker. Gingerbread men, called "gingerbread husbands," were the fashion then, and slabs of gingerbread were even gilded with gold. Honey was originally used to sweeten the dough; later sugar and molasses were introduced.

The English carried their taste for ginger to America. Ginger cookies were passed out to voters, and ginger was included in the rations of American soliders during the Revolution. Crystallized ginger, considered an aid to digestion, was nibbled at the end of a meal.

Today ginger is used in both savory and sweet dishes in many cultures around the world. In Asia it is believed to provide a yang counterpoint to milder yin ingredients. Essential in Chinese cooking, ginger enhances everything from soup to sweets and is almost always used with fish, as it is thought to ensure a fresh taste. In Japan, pickled ginger is a familiar condiment for sushi, while fresh ginger seasons marinades, soups, and dipping sauces. Korean cooks use ginger in grilled meats, salads, and kimchee. In Southeast Asia, fresh ginger imbues innumerable noodle dishes, curries, stir-fries, and salads. In the Middle East and North Africa, ground ginger heightens curries and *tagines*. In Thailand, the flowers are eaten fried as we relish zucchini flowers. In Europe, ginger is primarily used in sweets such as gingersnaps, ginger ale, ginger beer, and cakes.

As East meets West in America, innovative chefs are using ginger in a wide variety of dishes: seafood appetizers, fruit salads, vegetable soups, grilled meats and fish, vegetable side dishes, chutneys and condiments, and baked and frozen desserts. Ginger is a natural for low-fat cooking, as it is one of the few spices that needs no fat to carry its racy flavor, and its fresh taste and versatility guarantee it a place in this country's developing cuisine.

cooking with ginger

Ginger is available fresh, dried in slices, ground, pickled in sweet rice vinegar, preserved in sugar syrup, and crystallized or candied and sugar-coated.

buying fresh ginger

Fresh ginger is available in two types. Young, or baby, ginger has a soft, thin, pink-tinged translucent skin and a green-tinged pale ivory flesh. Sometimes called green ginger, it is best pickled, preserved in syrup, or candied. Usually available for only a brief season in spring to early summer, it is expensive and less pungent in flavor but less fibrous in texture than mature ginger. Traditional ginger, available year around, has a light beige to tan skin and a pale golden to creamy flesh. Mature rhizomes are more fibrous and hotter in flavor than younger ones. It is difficult to judge maturity without slicing into the rhizome, though you can check the fibers that protrude from a freshly cut knob.

Select a hand, or "race" that is unblemished, firm, and heavy, signifying freshness. A shiny look is not necessarily a sign of freshness, as the appearance of the skin can vary with the country of origin. Avoid dry or shriveled stems that feel light for their size.

storing ginger

At home ginger is best stored in a plastic bag in the vegetable crisper, wrapped in a paper towel to absorb any moisture that might encourage mildew. It will keep for two to three weeks or longer, depending on its freshness at the time of purchase. For long-term storage, cut the ginger in 1-inch sections, peel them, place them in a small jar and add enough sherry to cover. The sherry also comes in handy for stir-fries and other cooking. Freezing is acceptable if the ginger is to be grated or blended, because freezing will make it mushy.

Store ground ginger in a cool, dry, dark place and replace it after six months.

preparing fresh ginger

⊚ To peel, use a potato peeler to strip off the tan skin. It usually is not necessary to peel the thin skin of young ginger.

⊚ To slice, thinly cut across the fibers of the knob with a large knife.

⊚ To julienne, cut ⅛-inch-thick slices of ginger across the grain. Stack a few at a time and cut into matchstick pieces.

⊚ To mince, cut into julienne strips, then cut again to make a fine dice. A food processor is not good to use here as it can smash or tear ginger.

⊚ To grate, use a stainless steel, aluminum, or porcelain grater, available at stores carrying Asian cookware.

⊚ To juice, grate the ginger onto cheesecloth, then wrap the cloth around the grated ginger and squeeze over a bowl.

Hands or slices of ginger are available in dried form in specialty Asian markets, ready to be freshly ground in a spice grinder. Ground ginger is abundantly available in spice jars. Stem ginger preserved in syrup often comes packed in glazed pottery or green crocks. Preserved, pickled, and crystallized ginger are available commercially in Asian and specialty foods markets. To make pickled ginger, see page 18; for crystallized ginger, see page 66.

E.H

Appetizers

Soups, &

Salads

pickled ginger

ⓢ

With its fine texture and mild flavor, young ginger makes sprightly pickled wafers to accompany seafood appetizers or just to nibble on. Select long, slender knobs for ease in slicing.

4 ounces fresh young ginger, peeled

1/4 cup sugar

1 cup rice vinegar

1 teaspoon salt

Using a sharp knife, cut the ginger crosswise against the grain into wafer-thin slices. Place in a bowl, pour boiling water over to cover, and let stand for 2 minutes; drain.

In a saucepan, bring the sugar, vinegar, and salt to a boil while stirring, and heat just until the sugar is dissolved. Pour mixture over the ginger, let cool, and transfer to a glass jar. Refrigerate for 1 day before using. The ginger will turn pale pink. It will keep for several months.

makes about 3/4 cup

E.H

gingered appetizer patties

*These robustly seasoned low-fat meat patties are good hot or cold. A small scoop
makes a handy tool for shaping the patties.*

Preheat the broiler. In a medium bowl, mix together the ground meat, shallot, garlic, parsley, ginger, allspice, salt and pepper, wine, and 1 tablespoon of the mustard. With a small scoop (1^1/$_4$ inches in diameter) or 2 spoons, shape the mixture into small patties. Place on a sheet of aluminum foil on the broiler rack and pat to a ^{1}/$_2$-inch thickness. Place the broiler rack about 4 inches from the heat and broil for about 4 minutes on each side, or until just cooked through. Spread the patties with mustard, top each with a sun-dried tomato half and a sliver of cheese, and return to the broiler just until the cheese melts, about 1 minute. Top each patty with an arugula sprig. Serve hot or cold as a hearty out-of-hand snack or on toasted baguette slices.

1 pound ground turkey, chicken, or lean pork

1 shallot, chopped

2 garlic cloves, minced

2 tablespoons chopped fresh flat-leaf (Italian) parsley

1 tablespoon minced fresh ginger

^{1}/$_2$ teaspoon ground allspice

salt and freshly ground black pepper to taste

^{1}/$_4$ cup dry red wine or dry sherry

3 tablespoons Dijon or stone-ground mustard

18 soft sun-dried tomatoes

3 ounces regular or low-fat Jarlsberg cheese, thinly sliced

18 arugula sprigs

toasted baguette slices (optional)

makes 18 appetizers

ginger singing scallops

﹫

This appetizer has everything going for it: It's fresh, fast, and fun to serve. Preparation takes less than 10 minutes. Scallop shells make a handsome serving container for these bite-sized morsels. If available, singing scallops from Northwest waters provide pretty pink or rosy-hued shells in an ideal diminutive size.

GINGER DIPPING SAUCE

3 tablespoons dry sherry

1 tablespoon light soy sauce

2 teaspoons minced fresh ginger

1 garlic clove, minced

1 teaspoon minced fresh chives

dash chili oil (optional)

2 tablespoons olive oil

1 garlic clove, minced

2 teaspoons minced fresh ginger

6 ounces singing scallops or bay
  scallops

TO MAKE THE GINGER DIPPING SAUCE: In a small bowl, stir together all the dipping sauce ingredients. Place the bowl in the center of a serving platter.

In a medium skillet, heat the oil and stir-fry the garlic and ginger for 1 minute. Add the scallops and stir-fry until barely cooked through and opaque, about 1 minute. Transfer each scallop to a scallop shell and skewer with a toothpick. Arrange the shells on the platter and let guests dip the scallops into the sauce.

VARIATION: If desired, 8 ounces large shrimp can substitute for the scallops. Peel and devein the shrimp, leaving on the tails, then sauté in the oil with the ginger and garlic for 2 to 3 minutes, or until the shrimp turn pink. Serve with dipping sauce.

makes about 3 dozen appetizers

curried fresh tomato soup

❀

This scarlet soup spiced with curry and ginger has a cool yogurt and herb garnish.

1 tablespoon olive oil

1 large onion, chopped

1 garlic clove, minced

1 teaspoon curry powder

1 tablespoon minced fresh ginger

6 tomatoes, peeled, or 1 can (15 ounces) whole tomatoes

1 can (6 ounces) tomato paste

2 cups homemade or canned low-salt chicken broth

1 tablespoon fresh lemon juice or white wine vinegar

salt and freshly ground black pepper to taste

plain yogurt and fresh flat-leaf (Italian) parsley or basil sprigs or diced avocado

In a large saucepan, heat the oil and sauté the onion, garlic, curry powder, and ginger until the onion is translucent, about 5 minutes. Add the tomatoes, tomato paste, and chicken broth. Cover and simmer for 30 minutes. Let cool slightly. In a blender or food processor, puree the mixture in batches with the lemon juice or vinegar. Season with salt and pepper. Serve hot or cold in soup bowls, garnished with a spoonful of yogurt and parsley, basil, or avocado.

makes 6 servings

ginger-carrot soup

🌀

This bright orange soup gets a special fillip from ginger.

In a large saucepan, place the chicken broth, onion, carrots, nutmeg, ginger, garlic, and pepper seasoning. Cover and simmer until the vegetables are very tender, about 20 minutes. Let cool slightly and puree in a blender or a food processor. Season with salt and pepper to taste. Return to the saucepan, stir in the wine, and heat through. Ladle into bowls and garnish with parsley, chives, or apple.

makes 4 servings

3 cups homemade or canned low-
   salt chicken broth
1 large sweet onion, chopped
4 large carrots, peeled and cut into
   1-inch chunks
1/8 teaspoon ground nutmeg
2 teaspoons minced fresh ginger
1 garlic clove, minced
dash liquid hot pepper seasoning
salt and freshly ground pepper
   to taste
1/4 cup dry white wine
chopped fresh flat-leaf (Italian)
   parsley, fresh chives, or diced
   red apple

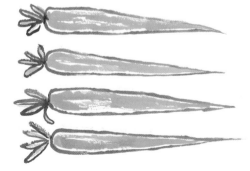

avocado halves with shrimp and jícama salad

This summery salad plate stems from a sojourn to Manzanillo Bay in Mexico. There a seaside picnic in a cove overlooking the sparkling water included this among other sumptuous seafood plates. Replace the avocado with fresh mango or papaya for another variation.

GINGER VINAIGRETTE

2 tablespoons olive oil

1 teaspoon Dijon or stone-ground mustard

3 tablespoons fresh lemon or lime juice

1 teaspoon grated lemon or lime zest

2 teaspoons minced fresh ginger

1 green onion (white part only), chopped

2 tablespoons chopped fresh cilantro

1 small garlic clove, minced

10 ounces small cooked bay shrimp

1 cup diced peeled jícama

1 small red bell pepper, halved, cored, seeded, and diced

2 tablespoons chopped green onion tops

butter lettuce

2 avocados, peeled, halved, and pitted; or 1 large papaya, halved, seeded, and quartered; or 2 mangoes, peeled and sliced

To MAKE THE GINGER VINAIGRETTE: In a small bowl, mix together all of the vinaigrette ingredients.

In a small bowl, toss together the shrimp, jícama, bell pepper, and onion tops. Pour dressing over the salad and mix lightly. Line 4 plates with lettuce leaves and center each with an avocado half, papaya quarter, or mango slices. Spoon the shrimp salad onto the avocado, papaya, or mango.

makes 4 servings

Ginger Root

chinese chicken and fruit salad

Kiwifruit, oranges, and strawberries are refreshing additions to a chicken salad with ginger-sesame dressing.

GINGER-SESAME DRESSING

1 tablespoon canola oil

1 1/2 tablespoons light soy sauce

1 tablespoon dark sesame oil

1 tablespoon honey

1 tablespoon fresh lemon or lime juice

1 teaspoon lemon or lime zest

1 tablespoon grated fresh ginger

dash liquid hot pepper seasoning (optional)

2 cooked chicken breast halves

1 celery stalk, thinly sliced on the diagonal

1/2 cup diced peeled jícama

butter lettuce or mixed salad greens

2 navel oranges, thinly sliced

2 kiwifruit, peeled and thinly sliced

1/2 cup strawberries, hulled

2 tablespoons toasted slivered almonds or
  pistachios

TO MAKE THE GINGER-SESAME DRESSING: In a bowl, combine all of the dressing ingredients.

Skin and bone the chicken and tear the meat into strips. Place the meat in a medium bowl with the celery and jícama, and mix with the dressing. Arrange the lettuce leaves on 2 plates and spoon chicken salad in a mound in the center of each. Ring with the oranges, kiwifruit, and berries. Sprinkle with the nuts.

makes 2 servings

gingered slaw

A spicy, fruity dressing cloaks a colorful, low-fat slaw that is ideal for a buffet, potluck, or picnic.

With a vegetable peeler, peel off the zest of the oranges, then peel off the white pith and discard it. In a food processor or blender, shred the oranges, orange zest, carrots, cabbage, apples, parsley, onion, and oregano, if desired. In a large bowl, stir together the chutney, ginger, vinegar, oil, and mustard. Add the slaw and mix to coat. Cover and chill. This is best if served within 2 days.

makes about 6 cups

NOTE: For an attractive presentation, serve the slaw on a bed of red leaf lettuce, curly endive, or arugula and ring the platter with sliced oranges.

2 oranges, unpeeled and quartered

2 carrots, peeled and coarsely chopped

one fourth of 1 large head green cabbage, coarsely chopped

2 Granny Smith apples, cored and quartered

2 tablespoons fresh flat-leaf (Italian) parsley

1 green onion, coarsely chopped

1 tablespoon fresh oregano (optional)

3 tablespoons chutney

2 teaspoons minced fresh ginger

2 tablespoons red wine vinegar or raspberry vinegar

1 tablespoon dark sesame oil

2 teaspoons Dijon mustard

curried brown rice and fruit salad

◎

Tart fruit chunks and dried cranberries lace this spicy rice with a refreshing tang, and pistachios lend a contrasting color and crunch. Serve warm or at room temperature.

2 cups water

1 cup long-grain brown rice

1 tablespoon curry powder

2 teaspoons minced fresh ginger

$1/4$ teaspoon each ground ginger and
   allspice

$3/4$ teaspoon salt

2 teaspoons canola oil

3 tablespoons dried cranberries or
   currants

3 tablespoons chopped pistachio nuts
   or peanuts

1 green onion, finely chopped

3 kiwifruit

2 red Bartlett pears or red apples

butter lettuce or other greens

In a medium saucepan, bring the water to a boil and stir in the rice, curry powder, fresh and ground ginger, allspice, salt, and oil. Cover and simmer for 35 minutes, or until the water is absorbed. Let cool slightly. Lightly stir in the cranberries or currants, nuts, and onion. Peel the kiwifruit; dice 1 fruit and slice 2. Quarter and core the pears or apples; dice 1 fruit and slice the other. Mix the diced fruit into the rice salad. Arrange the greens on plates and spoon the salad on top. Garnish with overlapping slices of pear or apple and kiwifruit.

makes 4 servings

fruit salad bowls with ginger-honey dressing

ↄ

Cantaloupe quarters make neat, edible serving bowls for this refreshing salad or light dessert.

Cut the melon into quarters and scoop out the seeds. In a bowl, mix together the grapes, berries, banana, and nectarine or peach.

TO MAKE THE GINGER-HONEY DRESSING: In a small bowl, stir together all the dressing ingredients. Pour over the fruits and mix lightly. Spoon onto the melon boats. Serve at once.

makes 4 servings

NOTE: The fruit selection can vary to suit the availability. Other options include a tropical selection such as kiwifruit, mango, star fruit, and pineapple.

1 medium cantaloupe

1 cup seedless green or red grapes

1 cup strawberries, hulled

1 banana, thinly sliced

1 nectarine or white peach, sliced

GINGER-HONEY DRESSING

1/4 cup honey

1/4 cup fresh lime juice

1 teaspoon grated lime zest

2 teaspoons grated fresh ginger

Entrées

and

Accompaniments

ginger fettuccine with shrimp and sugar snap peas

This colorful seafood pasta goes together in a jiffy. If fresh lemongrass is available, add 1 teaspoon finely chopped for an elusive tang. Accompany this dish with a mesclun *salad and papaya boats, melon wedges, or mango slices.*

6 ounces fresh or dried fettuccine or other pasta

2 tablespoons olive oil

2 green onions, cut into 1/2-inch pieces

2 teaspoons grated fresh ginger

1 garlic clove, minced

8 ounces medium raw shrimp, peeled, slit lengthwise, and deveined

4 ounces sugar snap peas or Chinese snow peas, trimmed

1/2 cup diced peeled jícama or sliced water chestnuts

8 small white mushrooms, sliced

1/3 cup clam juice or homemade or canned low-fat chicken broth

1 teaspoon *each* cornstarch and cold water

1 teaspoon soy sauce

dash hot pepper seasoning, if desired

fresh cilantro, basil, or flat-leaf (Italian) parsley sprigs for garnish

In a large pot, cook the pasta in boiling salted water until al dente, about 3 to 4 minutes for fresh pasta or 8 to 10 minutes for dried; drain.

Meanwhile, in a wok or large skillet, heat the oil. Add the onions, ginger, and garlic, and stir-fry for 2 to 3 minutes, or until translucent. Add the shrimp and sauté until it turns pink. Stir in the sugar snap peas, jícama or water chestnuts, mushrooms, and clam juice or chicken broth, and let cook for 1 minute, stirring. Blend together the cornstarch, cold water, soy sauce, and pepper seasoning, if desired, and stir in. Cook, stirring until thickened. Pour over the pasta and mix lightly. Serve on hot plates and garnish with herb sprigs.

makes 2 servings

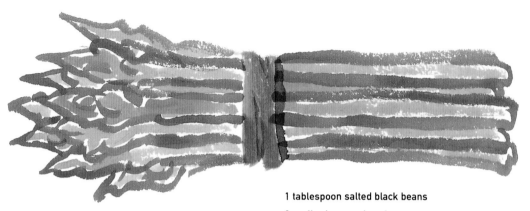

1 tablespoon salted black beans

2 garlic cloves, minced

1 tablespoon minced fresh ginger

2 teaspoons cornstarch

1 tablespoon water

1 teaspoon oyster sauce (optional)

$1/2$ teaspoon dark sesame oil

2 tablespoons peanut or vegetable oil

6 ounces shrimp, peeled and deveined

2 green onions, chopped

12 ounces asparagus, cut into 1-inch-long diagonal
slices, blanched for 1 minute

$1/2$ cup homemade or canned low-salt chicken broth

1 tablespoon light soy sauce

Hot steamed rice

stir-fried asparagus and shrimp with black bean sauce

A tiny Vietnamese-Chinese restaurant in Palo Alto, California, serves eye-catching platters of this succulent, spicy dish. When asparagus is out of season, long beans stand in. Salted, or fermented, black beans are a staple Chinese ingredient available in plastic packages in Asian markets. Refrigerate or freeze the beans for storing long term.

In a small bowl, cover the black beans with warm water; let soak for 1 minute, then drain and rinse thoroughly to remove salt. Put in a bowl with the garlic and ginger; mash into a paste and set aside. In a small bowl, mix together the cornstarch and water. Add the optional oyster sauce and the sesame oil; stir to a smooth paste and set aside.

Heat a wok or large skillet over medium high heat, add 1 tablespoon of the oil, then add the shrimp and stir-fry until they turn pink. Remove and set aside. To the hot pan, add the remaining 1 tablespoon oil and the black bean paste and stir-fry for several seconds, or until the mixture is fragrant. Toss in the onions, stir-fry for 10 seconds, then add the asparagus in 2 or 3 batches, a few seconds apart, making certain the wok is hot enough before adding more. Pour in the broth, add the soy sauce, and bring to a boil. If the asparagus needs more cooking, cover the wok for 1 minute. Stir the cornstarch mixture, and when the asparagus is crisp-tender, add the mixture to the center of the wok and stir until thickened, about 1 minute. Return the shrimp to the pan, stir and heat through, and serve at once with rice alongside.

makes 2 entrées

steamed whole fish with ginger

ඉ

*A splendid way to cook a whole fish is by steaming it Chinese style, strewn with
ginger and green onions and splashed with soy sauce and sherry. A large wok,
16 to 18 inches in diameter, makes an ideal steamer when fitted with a rack.*

1 fresh white-fleshed fish, about 1 1/2
   pounds (rock cod, sheepshead, red
   snapper, or sea bass)

1 green onion

2 tablespoons dry sherry

2 teaspoons light soy sauce

1/2 teaspoon dark sesame oil

1 tablespoon canola oil

1 tablespoon minced fresh ginger

fresh cilantro sprigs for garnish

Rinse the fish and pat dry. Place on a heatproof
platter. Chop the white part of the green onion;
cut the green part into 1-inch lengths and sliver
them into narrow strips. Mix together the sherry,
soy sauce, sesame oil, canola oil, and ginger and
set aside. Pour enough water into a wok or
steamer to come within 1 inch of the rack. Cover
and bring to a boil. Place the platter of fish on
the rack, pour the sauce over the sauce, and
strew the onion decoratively on top. Cover and
steam for 15 to 20 minutes, or until the fish is just
firm to the touch. Garnish with the cilantro
sprigs and serve whole. At the table, peel back
the skin and fillet the fish from the bones to
serve.

makes 2 to 3 servings

gingered fish fillets pacific

Emerald green kiwifruit or tropical star fruit makes a striking still life with pale pink fish fillets in this East/West seafood dish.

In a nonaluminum dish, stir together the sherry, soy sauce, lemon or lime juice, garlic, and ginger. Turn the fish fillets in the marinade, cover, and let stand for 15 minutes. Meanwhile, preheat the broiler. Place the fish on a broiling pan and broil 4 inches from the heat for 4 to 5 minutes, or until the fish flakes when poked with a fork, spooning some marinade over the fish halfway through the cooking. Garnish each serving with a few slices of fruit.

2 tablespoons dry sherry

1 tablespoon soy sauce

2 teaspoons fresh lemon or lime juice

1 garlic clove, minced

2 teaspoons minced fresh ginger

2 salmon, trout, or turbot fillets, about 8 ounces

sliced kiwifruit, star fruit, papaya, or orange for garnish

makes 2 servings

NOTE: Salmon trout fillets are excellent in this recipe as well.

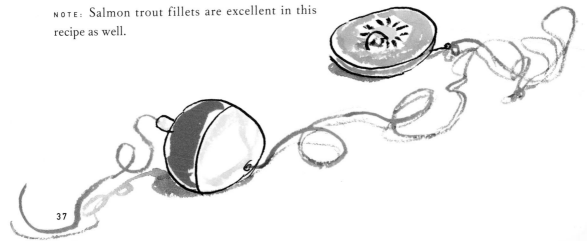

indian eggplant slices

A brilliant combination of flavors, colors, and temperatures, this old favorite is shared by an artist friend, Krishna Kopell.

Preheat the oven to 425°F. In a saucepan, sauté the onion in the oil until soft and translucent, about 5 minutes. Add the tomato paste, tomatoes, ginger, salt, and pepper; cover and simmer for 20 minutes. Meanwhile, slice the eggplant 1 inch thick, brush both sides lightly with oil, and place the slices on a baking sheet. Cover with aluminum foil. Bake in the oven for 20 to 30 minutes, turning once, or until the eggplant is cooked through. Transfer to a serving platter. Spoon the hot tomato sauce over the eggplant and top with the yogurt. Garnish with arugula or cilantro sprigs.

1 small onion, finely chopped

1 tablespoon olive oil

1/4 cup tomato paste

4 Roma (pear) tomatoes, diced

2 teaspoons minced fresh ginger

Salt and freshly ground black
   pepper to taste

1 small eggplant

olive oil for coating

1 cup plain low-fat yogurt

fresh arugula or cilantro sprigs
   for garnish

makes 4 servings

five-spice roast game hens with tropical fruit

꩜

Chinese five-spice powder is a blend of cinnamon, cloves, fennel seed, star anise, and Szechuan peppercorns. Combined with ginger and added to a soy sauce marinade, it gives a zesty taste to little hens served with fruit and lime wedges.

2 Cornish game hens, about 1 pound 6 ounces each, or 4 chicken drumstick and thigh quarters

1/4 teaspoon freshly ground black pepper

1 teaspoon Chinese five-spice powder

2 tablespoons soy sauce

2 tablespoons dry sherry

2 teaspoons minced fresh ginger

1 garlic clove, minced

1 teaspoon dark sesame oil

1 kiwifruit, star fruit, or tangerine, peeled and sliced or sectioned

1 lime, cut into wedges

Preheat the oven to 375°F. Remove the giblets from the game hens; rinse the hens or chicken quarters and pat dry. Rub the hens or quarters with pepper and five-spice powder and place on a rack in a roasting pan. Roast in the oven for 15 minutes. Mix together the soy sauce, sherry, ginger, garlic, and oil, and brush this basting sauce over the birds. Roast the chicken quarters 30 minutes longer and the hens 45 minutes longer, or until the drumsticks move easily in their joints. To serve, cut each hen in half; garnish each serving with a few slices of fruit and accompany with a lime wedge.

makes 4 servings

flank steak teriyaki

◉

A tangy marinade adds depth and flavor to this steak, making it a winning entrée. Grill red onion rings to serve alongside. Combine leftover meat and wholegrain bread for a hearty sandwich.

In a shallow nonaluminum pan, mix together the soy sauce, honey, vinegar, garlic, ginger, and onion. Turn the meat in the marinade, cover, and refrigerate; marinate several hours or overnight, turning once or twice. Let meat warm to room temperature for 30 minutes before cooking. Broil or grill for about 4 minutes on each side for medium-rare. Slice thinly on the diagonal.

3 tablespoons soy sauce

2 tablespoons honey

1 1/2 tablespoons red wine vinegar

1 garlic clove. minced

2 teaspoons minced fresh ginger

1 green onion (white part only). chopped

1 flank steak or top sirloin (about 1 1/2 pounds)

makes 4 servings

Er. H

41

gingered pork tenderloin

Glazed pork tenderloin is an ideal entrée for entertaining; boneless turkey breast works especially well in this recipe. Serve warm or chilled to suit the season and accompany with Gingered Fruit Salsa (page 46) and a brown rice casserole or tabbouleh salad.

one 2-pound pork tenderloin or
   boneless turkey breast
2 garlic cloves, slivered
1 teaspoon green peppercorns
2 tablespoons Dijon mustard
1 tablespoon light soy sauce
1 teaspoon minced fresh ginger
1/4 teaspoon ground allspice
fresh watercress or flat-leaf (Italian)
   parsley sprigs
candied kumquats (optional)

Preheat the oven to 325°F. Make slashes in the pork or turkey and stud with the garlic and peppercorns. Mix together the mustard, soy sauce, ginger, and allspice, and spread over the surface of the meat. Place on a rack in a roasting pan and roast in the oven for 45 minutes to 1 hour, or until the internal temperature registers 165°F. Remove to a platter and serve warm or chilled, garnished with watercress or parsley, and candied kumquats cut like a flower, if desired.

makes 6 to 8 servings

gingered apricot chutney

A tangy ginger chutney is wonderful with curries and a great addition to grilled meats and poultry. If you love apricots, this is a good way to enjoy them all year long.

In a large, heavy pot, combine all the ingredients and simmer, uncovered, until the fruit is translucent and thick, about 30 minutes. Ladle into sterilized jars, cap, and seal. Refrigerate for up to 2 weeks, freeze, or process in a boiling water bath for longer storage.

makes about 6 cups

8 cups diced apricots or plums

1 large onion, chopped

2 garlic cloves, minced

1/4 cup minced fresh ginger

3/4 cup firmly packed brown sugar

1 1/2 cups cider vinegar

2 teaspoons mustard seeds

3/4 teaspoon salt

2 cinnamon sticks

1 teaspoon *each* ground cardamom
   and allspice

tiny piece dried red pepper

6 small flour tortillas

2 green onions

2 tablespoons canola oil

2 teaspoons dark sesame oil

6 ounces pork tenderloin or boneless chicken or
turkey breast, cut into $1/8$ inch-thick strips

2 teaspoons minced fresh ginger

1 garlic clove, minced

4 ounces white mushrooms or stemmed shiitake
mushrooms, sliced

$1/2$ cup sliced peeled jícama or water chestnuts

1 inner stalk celery, thinly sliced on the diagonal

1 tablespoon light soy sauce

1 tablespoon rice wine vinegar

2 eggs, lightly beaten

mu shu pork

Tuck this quick Asian stir-fry into flour tortillas for a family supper or brunch dish.

Preheat the oven to 350°F. Wrap the tortillas in aluminum foil and heat them in the oven for 10 minutes. Chop the white part of the onions. Cut the green stems into 1¹/₂-inch lengths, then make several ¹/₄-inch slashes in one end of each one, place the stems in a bowl of ice water, and let stand 5 to 10 minutes to fan out.

In a large nonstick skillet, heat 1¹/₂ tablepoons of the canola oil and the sesame oil. Add the pork, chicken, or turkey, chopped whites of the onions, and ginger, and stir-fry 1 minute. Add the garlic, mushrooms,

jícama or water chestnuts, and celery, and stir-fry for 1 minute. Add the soy sauce and vinegar, and heat, stirring to scrape up the cooking juices on the bottom of the pan.

In a small skillet, heat the remaining ¹/₂ tablespoon canola oil. Pour in the beaten eggs and scramble until barely set. Spoon the eggs onto a serving dish, cover with the meat mixture, and surround with the onion fans. Serve with the hot tortillas and let each person fill them with the hot egg and meat mixture, then fold and enjoy.

makes 2 to 3 servings

gingered fruit salsa

This zestful salsa can be made with various fresh fruits. Serve as an accompaniment to Mexican bean and tortilla entrées or with grilled fish, pork, lamb, duck, or chicken.

2 cups diced peeled mango, papaya,
   nectarines, or peaches
1/2 cup diced red onion
1/2 cup diced red bell pepper or red
   seedless grapes
1/4 cup chopped fresh cilantro
2 tablespoons fresh lime juice
2 teaspoons grated fresh ginger
dash chili powder or 1 jalapeño,
   seeded and thinly sliced (optional)

In a medium bowl, place the mango, red onion, red pepper or grapes, cilantro, lime juice, ginger, and chili powder or jalapeño, if desired. Mix lightly. Cover and chill until serving time. This is best served the same day it is prepared.

makes about 3 cups

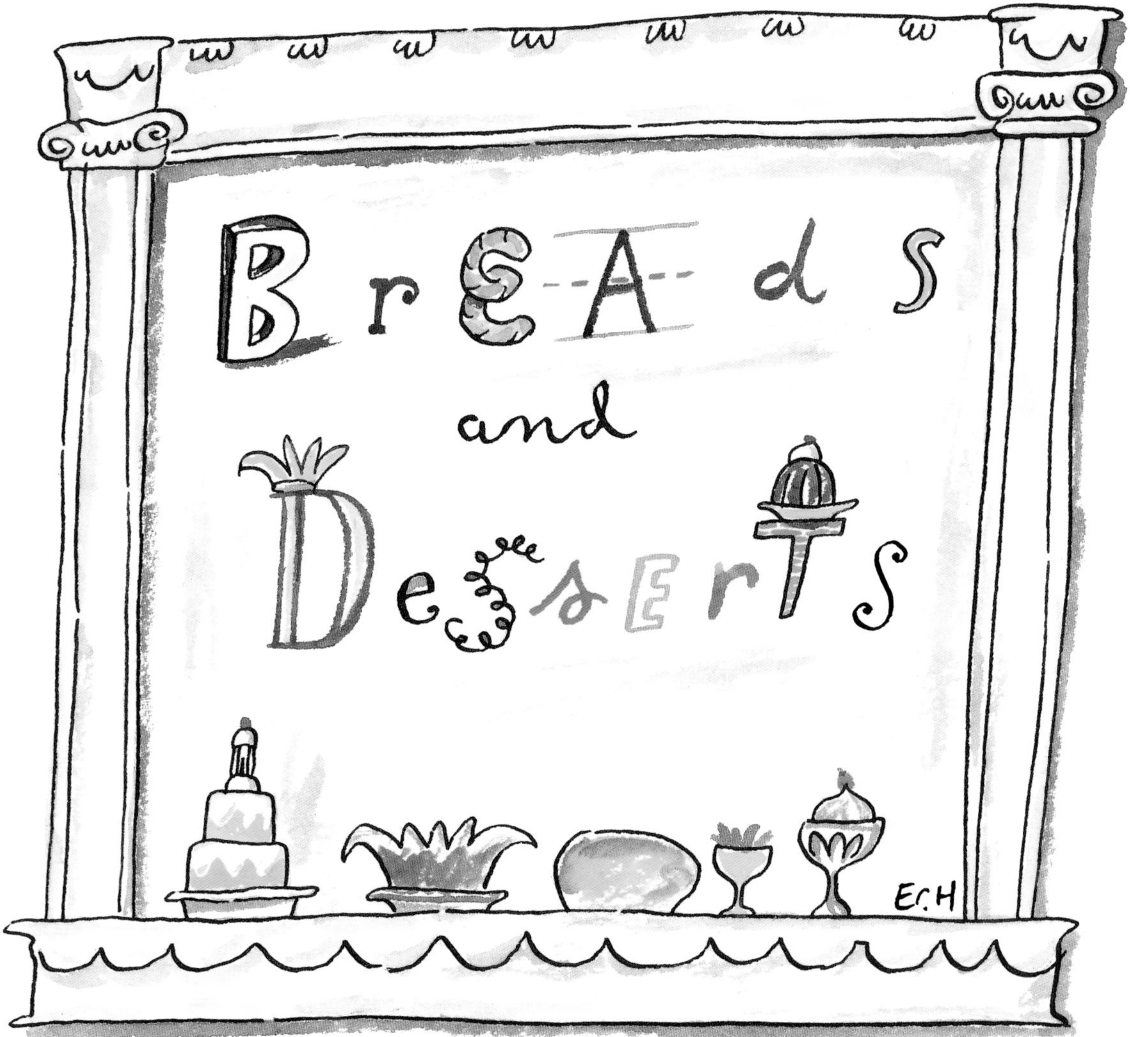
BrEAds
and
DesserTs
E.C.H

ginger smoothies

ᔓ

Vary this frosty drink with fruit in season for a wonderful morning meal. Top with wheat bran or muesli for extra fiber. For a single serving, simply halve the ingredients.

1 cup plain low-fat yogurt

one $1/4$-inch slice fresh ginger

1 banana, peeled and frozen in a plastic
   bag

2 navel oranges, peeled

$1/2$ cup frozen strawberries; or 1 frozen
   persimmon, peeled and diced; or 6
   frozen apricot halves

In a blender or food processor, place all of the ingredients and whirl until blended. Pour into tall glasses.

makes two 12-ounce servings

ginger-pecan bran muffins

Boosted with bran and without any added fat, these healthful muffins are delight-fully moist and fine-grained. Vary their flavor by adding fruit.

Preheat the oven to 350°F. Grease 12 large muffin cups. Place the nuts in a baking pan and bake in the oven for 8 minutes or until toasted. In a large bowl, stir together the flour, soda, salt, the ground and fresh ginger, brown sugar, wheat bran, and orange zest. Beat the egg with the buttermilk and molasses. Add to the dry ingredients and stir just until blended. Mix in the nuts. Using an ice cream scoop, scoop out mounds of batter and drop into the prepared muffin cups.

Bake in the oven for 20 to 25 minutes, or until golden brown and a toothpick inserted in the center of a muffin comes out clean. Let cool in the pan for 2 minutes, then remove the muffins to a rack or serving basket. Serve hot or reheat in a 350°F oven for 5 minutes or until heated through.

2/3 cup (3 ounces) chopped
    pecans or walnuts
2 cups unbleached all-purpose
    flour
1 1/2 teaspoons baking soda
1/2 teaspoon salt
1/2 teaspoon ground ginger
1 tablespoon minced fresh ginger
1/3 cup packed dark brown sugar
1 1/2 cups wheat bran
2 tablespoons coarsely grated
    orange zest
1 egg
1 1/2 cups buttermilk
1/4 cup dark molasses

makes 12 muffins

VARIATIONS: Add 1/2 cup frozen cranberries or blueberries, or 1/3 cup dried cranberries or currants to the batter.

down-under biscotti

⑤

These crispy wafers are a specialty of Australia, where they are called "toasts."
Santini Grilli, of Italian heritage and the co-proprietor of Primo Estate Winery,
located in the countryside of South Australia, served these cookies at a garden
wine tasting and gave me the recipe in grams. Nearby, in Adelaide, the Red
Ochre Grill bakes similar 10-inch-long cookies dotted with macadamia nuts to
complement honey and eucalyptus ice cream.

4 egg whites

dash salt

2/3 cup sugar

1/2 teaspoon ground ginger

1 tablespoon grated fresh ginger

1/4 teaspoon almond extract

1 teaspoon vanilla extract

1 1/4 cups unbleached all-purpose flour

1 1/4 cups (7 ounces) whole macadamia
nuts, blanched almonds, or peeled
hazelnuts

Preheat the oven to 300°F. Butter and flour a 9-inch square pan. In a large bowl, beat the egg whites and salt until soft peaks form, then gradually add the sugar and beat until stiff peaks form. Mix in the ground and fresh ginger, almond extract, and vanilla. Fold in the flour and nuts. Spread in the prepared pan. Bake in the middle of the oven for 30 minutes. Remove from the oven and turn out of the pan onto a rack; let cool 15 minutes. Slice as thinly as possible, about 3/16 inch thick, into long, slender slices. Lay flat on 2 baking sheets and return to a 150°F oven for 30 minutes. Turn off the oven and let the cookies dry in the oven 1 hour longer.

makes about 4 dozen long, slender cookies

triple-ginger cookies

Ginger in three forms brings an alluring spiciness to these crispy molasses cookies.

1/2 cup plus 2 tablespoons butter

1 cup firmly packed dark brown sugar

1/4 cup dark molasses

1 egg

2 1/4 cups unbleached all-purpose flour

2 teaspoons ground ginger

1 teaspoon baking soda

1/4 teaspoon salt

2 tablespoons minced fresh ginger

1/2 cup finely chopped crystallized
   ginger

1/2 cup (2 1/2 ounces) chopped blanched
   almonds

Preheat the oven to 350°F. In a large bowl, cream the butter and sugar until fluffy. Add the molasses and egg and beat until blended. In a medium bowl, stir together the flour, ground ginger, baking soda, and salt. Add to the creamed mixture and mix until smooth. Stir in the fresh and crystallized ginger and the nuts. Cover and chill for 1 hour. Pinch off small pieces of the dough and roll into 1-inch balls. Place on greased baking sheets. Bake in the middle of the oven for 10 minutes, or until golden brown. Transfer the cookies to wire racks to cool. Store in a tightly closed tin.

makes about 4 dozen cookies

old-fashioned gingersnaps

*At Stars, the celebrated San Francisco restaurant, pastry chef Emily Luchetti
times the baking of crackly-topped ginger cookies to present them still warm as
a finale to accompany coffee. Guests rave over their goodness, finding them more
appealing than a chocolate truffle. Owner Jeremiah Tower says the secret is to
serve them warm from the oven. This is my version of gingersnaps.*

Preheat the oven to 325°F. In a large bowl, beat the butter and sugars together until fluffy. Mix in the egg and molasses until smooth. In a medium bowl, stir together the flour, soda, salt, and spices. Add to the creamed mixture and mix until smooth. Chill for 1 hour. Spoon out rounded teaspoonfuls of dough and roll into balls. Roll in turbinado sugar to coat lightly. Place 2 inches apart on lightly greased baking sheets. Bake in the middle of the oven for 10 minutes, or just until browned on the edges and still barely soft in the center. Let cool slightly on a rack.

makes about 4 dozen cookies

3/4 cup (1 1/2 sticks) butter, at room
   temperature
1/2 cup *each* granulated and firmly
   packed brown sugar
1 egg
1/4 cup dark molasses
2 cups unbleached all-purpose
   flour
1 teaspoon baking soda
1/2 teaspoon salt
2 teaspoons ground ginger
1 teaspoon ground cinnamon
1/2 teaspoon ground cloves
turbinado sugar for coating

gingerbread cookies

⊚

*Snapping crisp and thin, these cookies are integral to the holiday season. Cut
them into little gingerbread men or into fancy shapes as bells, stars, ornaments,
and trees.*

Preheat the oven to 375°F. In a large bowl, cream the butter and sugar until fluffy. Mix in the egg, molasses, and vinegar, beating until smooth. In a medium bowl, stir together the remaining ingredients and mix in until blended. Chill for 1 hour. On a lightly floured board, roll out the dough 1/8 inch thick and cut out with floured decorative cutters. Place on lightly greased baking sheets. Bake in the middle of the oven for 6 to 8 minutes, or until golden brown on the edges. Remove cookies to a rack and let cool. Store in a tightly sealed container.

makes about 6 dozen cookies

1/2 cup (1 stick) butter at room
   temperature

3/4 cup packed brown sugar

1 egg

1/2 cup dark molasses

1 tablespoon cider vinegar

2 1/2 cups unbleached all-purpose
   flour

3/4 teaspoon baking soda

1/4 teaspoon salt

1 tablespoon ground ginger

1 teaspoon ground cinnamon

1/4 teaspoon *each* ground nutmeg
   and cloves

queensland ginger cake

۵

Queensland, Australia, is renowned for its choice fresh and crystallized ginger. While on a sojourn there and in New Zealand, I met cookbook author Shirley Bradstock of Christchurch, who shared this easy cake recipe. The cake is especially delectable served warm and topped with whipped cream and crystallized ginger.

1/3 cup butter, melted

3 tablespoons grated fresh ginger

1/2 cup honey

1/2 cup dark molasses

1/2 cup plain low-fat yogurt

1 egg

2 cups unbleached all-purpose flour

1 1/2 teaspoons baking soda

1/2 teaspoon dry mustard

1/2 teaspoon ground allspice

1/2 teaspoon ground cinnamon

whipped cream or frozen yogurt and
    chopped crystallized ginger (optional)

Preheat the oven to 375°F. Lightly butter and flour a 9-by-2-inch springform pan. In a large bowl, place the butter, ginger, honey, and molasses, and mix well. Mix in the yogurt and egg until smooth. In a medium bowl, stir together the flour, baking soda, mustard, allspice, and cinnamon. Add to the batter and mix until blended.

Pour the batter into the prepared pan. Bake in the middle of the oven for 30 to 35 minutes, or until a toothpick inserted in the center comes out clean. Let cool for 5 minutes on a rack, then turn out of the pan onto a rack. Serve warm or at room temperature, cut into wedges. Top with whipped cream or frozen yogurt and crystallized ginger, if desired.

makes one 9-inch round cake

ginger, carrot, and walnut cake

☙

This tender, buttery cake flaunts a trio of flavors: ginger, orange, and toasted walnuts.
It is ideal to make a day or two in advance and perfect for picnics and buffets.

Preheat the oven to 350°F. Grease and flour a 10-inch tube pan. Place the nuts in a baking pan and bake in the oven for 8 minutes, or until lightly toasted; let cool and chop finely. In a large bowl, beat the butter until creamy and gradually beat in the sugar. Add the eggs, one at a time, and beat until smooth. Mix in the orange zest, ginger, vanilla, and yogurt. In a small bowl, stir together the flour, baking powder, soda, salt, and ginger and stir into the creamed mixture, mixing until incorporated. Stir in the carrots and toasted nuts. Turn into the prepared pan.

Bake in the oven for 1 hour, or until a toothpick inserted in the center comes out clean. Invert the pan on a wire rack and let the cake cool completely. To serve, run a knife around the inside of the pan and invert the cake onto a cake plate. Remove the pan bottom and cut the cake into slices.

makes one 10-inch tube cake

3/4 cup (3 ounces) chopped walnuts

1 cup (2 sticks) butter at room temperature

1 1/2 cups sugar

4 eggs

grated zest of 1 orange

1 tablespoon minced fresh ginger

1 teaspoon vanilla extract

1 cup plain low-fat yogurt

2 1/2 cups unbleached all-purpose flour

1 teaspoon baking powder

1 teaspoon baking soda

1/4 teaspoon salt

1/2 teaspoon ground ginger

2 1/2 cups shredded carrots (about 4 carrots)

ginger-chocolate angel cake

A cocoa-flavored angel cake combines the best of two worlds: It is both light and rich in taste. For an indulgent embellishment, top it with Honey-Ginger Ice Cream (page 63) or chocolate frozen yogurt.

1 1/2 tablespooons minced fresh ginger (about 1 1/2 ounces)

1 1/2 cups plus 2 tablespoons sugar

1 2/3 cups egg whites (about 14) at
  room temperature

1 1/2 teaspoons cream of tartar

1/2 teaspoon salt

2 tablespoons water

1 1/2 teaspoons vanilla extract

1 cup cake flour

6 tablespoons unsweetened Dutch-
  process cocoa powder

Preheat the oven to 375°F. In a blender or food processor, place the ginger and 2 tablespoons of the sugar and process until finely minced; set aside. In a large bowl, beat the egg whites until frothy, then beat in the cream of tartar, salt, and water. Beat until soft peaks form, then gradually beat in 1 cup of the sugar and the vanilla, beating until stiff but not dry. Sift together the flour, remaining 1/2 cup sugar, and the cocoa. Gently fold this mixture into the egg whites along with the ginger-sugar mixture, mixing just until incorporated.

Turn the batter into an ungreased 10-inch tube pan. Bake in the middle of the oven for 40 minutes, or until a toothpick inserted in the center of the cake comes out clean. Invert the pan on a wire rack and let the cake cool completely. To serve, run a knife around the inside of the pan and invert the cake onto a cake plate. Remove the pan bottom and cut the cake into slices.

makes one 10-inch tube cake

ginger dacquiri ice with kiwifruit

This frosty ice is wonderfully refreshing served with slices of kiwifruit alongside.

2 teaspoons lime zest

6 tablespoons sugar

2 tablespoons minced fresh ginger

2 cups water

1/3 cup fresh lime juice

1/4 cup dark rum

2 kiwifruit

In a small bowl, mash the lime zest with 1/2 teaspoon of the sugar to bring out the essential oils. In a medium, heavy saucepan, place the remaining sugar, ginger, and water; bring to a boil, then reduce heat and simmer just until the sugar is dissolved. Remove from heat and let steep for 20 minutes; strain, discarding the ginger strands. Stir in the lime juice, rum, and lime zest. Pour into a shallow pan and freeze until solid, about 1 1/2 hours. Spoon into a food processor or mixing bowl and process or beat with an electric mixer until light and fluffy. Transfer to a plastic container and freeze until firm, or up to 1 week.

To serve, let soften in the refrigerator for 15 minutes, then spoon out and place in dessert bowls or balloon wineglasses. Peel and slice the kiwifruit and arrange alongside.

makes 1 1/2 pints

honey-ginger ice cream

A satiny ice cream is laced with the intriguing heat of ginger. Superb served as is, or top it with raspberries, blueberries, or strawberries.

In a small saucepan, place the water, sugar, and ginger, and simmer for 5 minutes; remove from heat and let cool. In a double boiler, beat the egg yolks slightly and stir in the honey, half-and-half, and ginger-sugar mixture. Place over simmering water and, stirring constantly, cook until the mixture has thickened enough to coat a spoon, about 10 to 15 minutes. Remove from heat and immediately place in a pan of ice-cold water to chill. Refrigerate until cold, or for several hours, if possible. Stir in the heavy cream and pour into a 2-quart ice cream maker. Freeze according to the manufacturer's directions. Serve at once, or freeze to hold until serving time. Let soften in the refrigerator for 15 minutes before serving. Spoon into dessert bowls or balloon wineglasses.

2/3 cup water

1/3 cup sugar

1/3 cup minced fresh ginger

6 egg yolks

3/4 cup honey

2 cups (1 pint) half-and-half

2 cups (1 pint) heavy (whipping) cream

makes about 1 3/4 quarts

NOTE: If the ginger is stringy after being cooked in the syrup, press it through a sieve and discard the pulp, then use the ginger syrup in the ice cream.

1 cup heavy (whipping) cream

1 cup half-and-half or milk

1 1/2 tablespoons minced fresh ginger

6 egg yolks

1/4 cup granulated sugar

1 teaspoon vanilla extract

2 tablespoons minced crystallized ginger

about 1/2 cup brown sugar

strawberries (optional)

ginger crème brûlée

☉

The spicy bite of ginger counters the sumptuous richness of this elegant dessert.
It is always a rewarding challenge to crack through the caramel disc and spoon
up the creamy custard. Fresh strawberries are a delightful accompaniment.

Preheat the oven to 300°F. In a medium saucepan, heat the cream and half-and-half or milk with the fresh ginger until scalded; remove from heat and let steep for 15 minutes, then strain, discarding the ginger. In a bowl, whisk the egg yolks until light and beat in the granulated sugar. Pour in a little of the cream and stir to blend. Stir in the vanilla and crystallized ginger. Pour into 6 buttered 4-ounce soufflé dishes. Place in a baking pan and add hot water to 1 inch up the sides of the dishes. Bake in the oven for 15 to 20 minutes, or until the custard is set. Remove from the oven.

Preheat the broiler. Spoon about $1/2$ cup of brown sugar into a sieve and, with the back of a spoon, push the sugar out to evenly coat the top of each custard with about 1 tablespoon of sugar. Place the baking pan with the custards in it under the broiler about 2 inches from the heat and broil just until the sugar melts and caramelizes, about 30 seconds. Remove the custards from the water bath and let cool at room temperature, or chill for up to 2 hours (after that time the topping may liquefy). Serve at room temperature or chilled with strawberries alongside, if desired.

makes 6 servings

crystallized ginger

Making your own crystallized ginger is a bit tedious but not difficult. This process is an adaptation of the instructions in Bruce Cost's cookbook **Ginger East to West.** *Chinese yellow rock sugar, available in Asian markets, adds a golden hue, but granulated sugar can substitute for it. Be certain to select fresh young ginger with a minimal fibrous texture.*

8 ounces fresh young ginger

$1/2$ cup granulated sugar

2 ounces (about 3 tablespoons) Chinese yellow rock sugar or granulated sugar

$3/4$ cup water

superfine sugar for coating (optional)

In a medium saucepan, place the ginger and cover with cold water; let stand overnight. Drain, cover with cold water, bring to a boil, and simmer, covered, for 10 minutes. Drain and let cool to room temperature. Peel the ginger and cut it into $1/8$-inch-thick slices. Place the slices in the saucepan, cover with water, and simmer for 10 minutes. Drain and cover again with water; simmer for 10 minutes and drain again.

Place the sugars in a heavy, medium saucepan with the $3/4$ cup water. Bring to a boil, reduce heat, and simmer until the sugar is dissolved. Add the ginger, bring to a boil, and simmer 5 minutes. Remove from heat and let stand for 1 hour. Then simmer gently for 30 minutes, or until the syrup is absorbed, stirring occasionally, then constantly for the last few minutes. Turn out onto waxed paper and let cool. If desired, toss the ginger lightly in superfine sugar. Store in a tightly closed container.

makes about 8 ounces ginger

NOTE: For a lovely confection, dip one half of the crystallized ginger slices in melted bittersweet chocolate and place on waxed paper until set.

index

table of equivalents

The exact equivalents in the following tables have been rounded for convenience.

OVEN TEMPERATURES

F.	Celsius	Gas
250	120	1/2
275	140	1
300	150	2
325	160	3
350	180	4
375	190	5
400	200	6
425	220	7
450	230	8
475	240	9
500	260	10

LIQUIDS

US	Metric	UK
2 tbl	30 ml	1 fl oz
1/4 cup	60 ml	2 fl oz
1/3 cup	80 ml	3 fl oz
1/2 cup	125 ml	4 fl oz
2/3 cup	160 ml	5 fl oz
3/4 cup	180 ml	6 fl oz
1 cup	250 ml	8 fl oz
1 1/2 cups	375 ml	12 fl oz
2 cups	500 ml	16 fl oz
4 cups/1 qt	1 liter	32 fl oz

US/UK

$oz = ounce$
$lb = pound$
$in = inch$
$ft = foot$
$tbl = tablespoon$
$fl\ oz = fluid\ ounce$
$qt = quart$

WEIGHTS

US/UK	Metric
1 oz	30 g
2 oz	60 g
3 oz	90 g
4 oz (1/4 lb)	125 g
5 oz (1/3 lb)	155 g
6 oz	185 g
7 oz	220 g
8 oz (1/2 lb)	250 g

US/UK	Metric
10 oz	315 g
12 oz (3/4 lb)	375 g
14 oz	440 g
16 oz (1 lb)	500 g
1 1/2 lb	750 g
2 lb	1 kg
3 lb	1.5 kg

METRIC

$g = gram$
$kg = kilogram$
$mm = millimeter$
$cm = centimeter$
$ml = milliliter$
$l = liter$

LENGTH MEASURES

1/8 in	3 mm
1/4 in	6 mm
1/2 in	12 mm
1 in	2.5 cm
2 in	5 cm
3 in	7.5 cm
4 in	10 cm
5 in	13 cm

6 in	15 cm
7 in	18 cm
8 in	20 cm
9 in	23 cm
10 in	25 cm
11 in	28 cm
12 in/1 ft	30 cm

a Pagoda

NORTH
AMERICA

Bermuda

GULF of
Mexico

Bahamas

Cuba - - - HISPANIOLA

Puerto

Jamaica

Caribbean
Sea

Curaçao

Trinidad
Tobago

Mexico

Baja

Central
America

Hawaii

SOUTH
AMERICA

Amazonia

Pacific

Fiji

Ocean

E.H